Iris Murdoch

THE IRISH WRITERS SERIES
James F. Carens, General Editor

EIMAR O'DUFFY	Robert Hogan
J. C. MANGAN	James Kilroy
J. M. SYNGE	Robin Skelton
PAUL VINCENT CARROLL	Paul A. Doyle
SEAN O'CASEY	Bernard Benstock
SEUMAS O'KELLY	George Brandon Saul
SHERIDAN LEFANU	Michael Begnal
SOMERVILLE AND ROSS	John Cronin
STANDISH O'GRADY	Phillip L. Marcus
SUSAN L. MITCHELL	Richard M. Kain
W. R. RODGERS	Darcy O'Brien
MERVYN WALL	Robert Hogan
LADY GREGORY	Hazard Adams
LIAM O'FLAHERTY	James O'Brien
MARIA EDGEWORTH	James Newcomer
SIR SAMUEL FERGUSON	Malcolm Brown
BRIAN FRIEL	D. E. S. Maxwell
PEADAR O'DONNELL	Grattan Freyer
DANIEL CORKERY	George Brandon Saul
BENEDICT KIELY	Daniel Casey
CHARLES ROBERT MATURIN	Robert E. Lougy
DOUGLAS HYDE	Gareth Dunleavy
EDNA O'BRIEN	Grace Eckley
FRANCIS STUART	J. H. Natterstad
JOHN BUTLER YEATS	Douglas N. Archibald
JOHN MONTAGUE	Frank Kersnowski
KATHARINE TYNAN	Marilyn Gaddis Rose
BRIAN MOORE	Jeanne Flood
PATRICK KAVANAGH	Darcy O'Brien
OLIVER ST. JOHN GOGARTY	J. B. Lyons
GEORGE FITZMAURICE	Arthur McGuinness

GEORGE RUSSELL (AE)	Richard M. Kain and James H. O'Brien
IRIS MURDOCH	Donna Gerstenberger
MARY LAVIN	Zack Bowen
FRANK O'CONNOR	James H. Matthews
ELIZABETH BOWEN	Edwin J. Kenney, Jr.
WILLIAM ALLINGHAM	Alan Warner
SEAMUS HEANEY	Robert Buttel
THOMAS DAVIS	Eileen Sullivan

IRIS MURDOCH

Donna Gerstenberger

Lewisburg
BUCKNELL UNIVERSITY PRESS
London: ASSOCIATED UNIVERSITY PRESSES

© 1975 by Associated University Presses, Inc.

Associated University Presses, Inc.
Cranbury, New Jersey 08512

Associated University Presses
108 New Bond Street
London W1Y OQX, England

Library of Congress Cataloging in Publication Data

Gerstenberger, Donna Lorine.
    Iris Murdoch.

    (The Irish writers series)
    Bibliography: p.
    1. Murdoch, Iris--Criticism and interpretation.
PR6063.U7Z66   1975   823'.9'14   74-126290
ISBN 0-8387-7774-0
ISBN 0-8387-7731-7 pbk.

Printed in the United States of America

Contents

Chronology		9
1	The Accomplishment	13
2	*The Red and the Green*	51
3	The Irish Connection	70
Selected Bibliography		80

Chronology

1919: Born in Dublin, July 15, daughter of Wills John Hughes Murdoch and Irene Alice Richardson. Education in England at Badminton School, Bristol.

1938-42: Somerville College, Oxford. First-class honors, classical "Greats."

1942-44: Assistant principal, Treasury.

1944-46: Administrative officer, UNRRA, working in London, Belgium, and Austria.

1947: Sarah Smithson studentship in philosophy, Newnham College, Cambridge.

1948: Appointment as Fellow of St. Anne's College, Oxford, and tutor in philosophy.

1953: *Sartre: Romantic Rationalist.*

1954: *Under the Net.*

1956: Marriage to John Oliver Bayley, fellow of New College, Oxford. *The Flight from the Enchanter.*

1957: *The Sandcastle.*

1958: *The Bell.*

1959: Visit to America to lecture at Yale University.

1961: *A Severed Head.* Dramatized with J. B. Priestly and performed 1963. Published 1964.

1962:   *An Unofficial Rose.*
1963:   *The Unicorn.*
1964:   *The Italian Girl.*
1965:   *The Red and the Green.*
1966:   *The Time of the Angels.*
1968:   *The Nice and the Good.*
1969:   *Bruno's Dream.*
1970:   *A Fairly Honourable Defeat. The Sovereignty of Good* and *The Servants and the Snow* (play).
1971:   *The Accidental Man.*
1973:   *The Black Prince.*

Iris Murdoch

1

The Accomplishment

We need more concepts than our philosophies have furnished us with.

—Iris Murdoch, "Against Darkness"

Although Iris Murdoch was born in Dublin within a few years of the Easter Rising and the caesarian birth pangs of modern Ireland and grew up with an awareness of Ireland's difficult definition and existence, her family life, her early schooling at Badminton, her employment by the English government and UNESCO, her training at Oxford and Cambridge, and her interest in modern continental philosophers have all contributed to the creation of a body of writing not particularly definable as Irish. If there are roots in her fiction, the main ones seem to be English, although the recurrence of Irish characters in Murdoch's novels and the extensive treatment of the Easter Rising in *The Red and the Green* make explicit a persistent consciousness of Ireland as a force in her fictional world. And there is, in all probability, a less direct but nonetheless real influence growing out of the Irish background in her treatment of setting and her choice of characters—both topics to be dealt with later in this study.

For the purposes of this introductory assessment of Murdoch's achievement, focus will not be on the question of her Irishness. Rather, I propose first of all to take a general look at the body of Murdoch's work, both literary and critical, and at her place in the world of modern fiction, before turning to a consideration of the specifically Irish aspect of her work. Among the reasons for this approach are the difficulties which readers and critics have had in finding a frame of reference in which to assess Murdoch's contribution to modern fiction, and whatever is to be said of her work as an Irish writer must share the same difficulties.

Among the readers of Iris Murdoch's novels are those who regard her almost annual production of a novel as confirmation of a truly fertile imagination and self-generating style. There are also those who see her as a writer who has given in to the tyranny of an "obsolete standard and . . . tired patterns (Linda Kuehl, "Iris Murdoch: The Novelist as Magician/The Magician as Artist," *Modern Fiction Studies* [Autumn 1969]). Beyond the question of frequency, the critical reception of Murdoch's novels has been dominated by those who insist on reading them for their philosophical statements or, in more recent years, for their elaborate mythic patterns. Even Murdoch's own critical statements have been valued primarily as they apply to her own practice of fiction, though she has produced eloquent and meaningful assessments of the state of the modern novel.

Part of the reason for the tendency to deal with Murdoch's work within one category or another is the very real difficulty of dealing with the intention (and tone) of individual novels: in categorization, the critic finds some comfort. Murdoch's novelistic structures are, by and large, traditional, her characters middle- or upper-middle class, their interactions largely polite, even when outrageous, their conversations often cerebral— even when the activity of a novel may be the bedding of all the characters in almost all possible combinations, as in *A Severed Head.*

Yet despite the familiar and traditional surfaces of Murdoch's fiction, the persistent use of which in the modern novel is its own kind of affront, her novels deal with the irrational in its various manifestations. The terrors of existence—which are, within Murdoch's traditional framework and under her objective, novelist's eye, rendered comic, pathetic, and ridiculous all at once—are delineated within the limits of her characters' apprehensions and reactions, whose own limitations necessarily circumscribe their range. That is to say, although some of Murdoch's ideas may be formally philosophical in origin, she is not primarily a philosophical novelist. Nor are her novels merely experimental formulations of her critical hypotheses, as some critics seem to expect them to be, although the novels do show a certain consonance with her ideas about what a novel ought to be like. It is much easier to say that Murdoch's novels are not some of the things that they have been thought to be than it is to say what they *are,* but because her fiction has had a persistently unsettling effect on reader and critic alike, it seems worth the

effort to try to get beyond the equations at which
evaluations of her work too often stop.

Murdoch's novels are, at their best, disturbing visions
of a disturbed world, visions that are rendered disturbing, in part, by the very formulations by which her
characters seek to hold the world at a distance, to come
to terms with it in some way. These structures often
remain within the realm of conventional manners or
consist of artificially imposed but societally acceptable
schemes (as in the religious communities of *The Bell*),
but, if the desperation or eccentricities are great enough,
the conventional may be inverted to invoke the darkness
itself (as in, among others, *The Flight from the
Enchanter, The Time of the Angels, The Italian Girl,* or
The Nice and the Good). The world that Murdoch
envisions is full of the fundamental absurdity that other
contemporary novelists have found at the center of their
universes, but the ways in which Murdoch has chosen to
render her fictional universe have been the source of
misunderstanding. The fact, for example, that Murdoch
has expressed admiration for and a desire to emulate
certain nineteenth-century novelists in their ability to
create characters with independence and distance from
their authors should not lead the reader to the conclusion that Murdoch is trying to revive the nineteenth-
century novel and succeeds or fails insofar as she is
successful in re-creating the tradition.

Speculations about the reasons for Murdoch's novelistic choices ought to begin with her own diagnosis of the
current condition of the novel and her own ideas about
ways in which to counter its all too obvious difficulties.
But the critic must keep always before him the

understanding of the distance between Murdoch's philosophical and critical ideas about fiction and her actual practice, which imposes, in fact, its own kind of limitations and ironies. Murdoch's essay, "Against Dryness: A Polemical Sketch" (*Encounter*) [January 1961]), is one of the most concise statements of her thinking about modern fiction, although her ideas are scattered throughout her essays and fiction—ideas which, beginning with the study of Sartre, have engaged her attention before and since the publication of her first novel.

Being "Against Dryness" does not argue for "wetness" (the terms seem to mean pretty much what they do in T. E. Hulme's *Speculations,* although he clearly argues the case in favor of classicism or "dryness"), for Murdoch has, in fiction and criticism, most cogently stated the dangers of romanticism in literature (and life). Dryness and romanticism both apply to ways in which the writer conceives and formulates the universe of his fiction, and dryness especially, as the prevailing modern mode, grows out of the inability of modern writers and thinkers to conceive widely or broadly or complexly enough about the totality of human experience. The "dry" writer is reductive; he substitutes complicated forms for the complexity of experience. He is, essentially, an avoider, although in part that which he avoids is what he is unable or unwilling to conceive. The background against which modern man lives and defines himself is monochromatic, if efficient, for as "heirs of the Enlightenment, Romanticism, and the Liberal tradition . . . we have been left with far too shallow and flimsy an idea of human personality."

The modern view of person sees man as defined only in behavioristic terms. His inner life is "identifiable as existing only through the application of it to public concepts, concepts which can only be constructed on the basis of overt behavior." Yet, because nothing transcends man, he is a solitary and totally free creature. "There is no transcendent reality, there are no degrees of freedom." Modern man casts no shadow. His empirical aims *have* been attainable and, paradoxically, this fact has resulted in the loss of a more complex world.

> We no longer use a spread-out substantial picture of the virtues of man and society. We no longer see man against a background of values, of realities, which transcend him. We picture man as a brave, naked will surrounded by an easily comprehended empirical world. For the hard idea of truth we have substituted a facile idea of sincerity.

The cost of this kind of freedom is the loss of background.

The reasons that Murdoch prefers the nineteenth-century novel to the novel of the twentieth century, which she sees as resembling that of the eighteenth, which was also an "era of rationalistic allegories and moral tales, the era when the idea of human nature was unitary and single," are that in the nineteenth century the structure of society was alive and complex and the novel was "not concerned with 'the human condition,' it was concerned with real various individuals struggling in society." Several years before her stand "Against Dryness," Murdoch had dealt with her preference for the nineteenth-century novel over the novel of the twentieth in an essay entitled "The Sublime and the Beautiful Revisited" (*Yale Review* [December 1959]), and the relationship between character and society is stated clearly. In the nineteenth-century

> The great novels are victims neither of convention nor of neurosis. The social scene is a life-giving framework and not a set of dead conventions or stereotyped setting inhabited by stock characters. And the individuals in the novels are free, independent of their author, and not merely puppets in the exteriorization of some closely locked psychological conflict of his own.

The richness of the nineteenth-century novel is lost in the twentieth century, for, she wrote in "Against Dryness," "the 20th-century novel is either crystalline or journalistic; that is, it is either a small quasi-allegorical object portraying the human condition and not containing 'characters' in the 19th-century sense, or else it is a large shapeless quasi-documentary object, the degenerate descendant of the 19th-century novel." Yet both the crystalline and the journalistic approaches to art are descendants of the Romantic tradition. Hulme's "dryness" which "is a nemesis of Romanticism," Murdoch sees quite rightly as "Romanticism in a later phase . . . the pure, clean, self-contained 'symbol' is what is left of the other-worldliness of Romanticism when the 'messy' humanitarian and revolutionary elements have spent their force." In both the crystalline and the journalistic, reality is avoided, and fantasy rather than imagination is enjoined. The difficulties of knowing the real world are altogether escaped, and the facile, dreamlike surface which we so efficiently substitute for "the difficulty and complexity of the moral life and the opacity of persons" denies the human potential for growth.

Only through literature is it possible to rediscover the density of human life: "We need to turn our attention away from the consoling dream necessity of Romanticism, away from the dry symbol, the bogus individual, the false whole, towards the real impenetrable human person."

To be "against dryness" is to respect the contingent, to move from fantasy to imagination. Form consoles us, but like our simple-minded faith in science it does so at a terrible cost, although, by and large, it is hard to conceive that which has been withdrawn.

> Against the consolations of form, the clear crystalline work, the simplified fantasy-myth, we must pit the destructive power of the now so unfashionable naturalistic idea of character . . . , [for] people are destructive of myth, contingency is destructive of fantasy. . . . Literature must always represent a battle between real people and images; and what it requires now is a much stronger and more complex conception of the former.

The ideas of "Against Dryness" explicate further ideas already present in Murdoch's earlier study *Sartre: Romantic Rationalist* (1953), in which she concludes that philosopher-novelist Jean-Paul Sartre fails as a novelist because of his fatal impatience with the *"stuff* of human life." The great novelist has what Sartre lacks, "an apprehension of the absurd irreducible uniqueness of people and their relations with each other." Although the hero of *La Nausée* discovers the contingency of experience and suffers disgust as a result of his discovery, Sartre as a novelist, like Murdoch herself in most novels, is unable to create a fictional world to embody contingency. Murdoch's painful awareness that

Sartre's "inability to write a great novel is a tragic symptom of a situation which afflicts us all. We know that the real lesson to be taught is that the human person is precious and unique; but we seem unable to set it forth except in terms of ideology and abstraction" is still present in the analysis of "Against Dryness," published in the same year as her fifth novel. Her first, *Under the Net,* was published a year after *Sartre: Romantic Rationalist,* and each subsequent novel has seemed a further attempt to grapple with the problems diagnosed in the book on Sartre and the essays following.

Yet Murdoch's novels are not philosophical novels in the sense that *La Nausée* may be said to be a philosophical working out of an idea, an exploration of a proposition, for it is the business of philosophy to say what was thought to be unsayable, not to embody forth the messy grounds, the primary condition about which philosophy speaks. *Under the Net* perhaps comes closest to this category of philosophical novel. In an interview with Frank Kermode, "The House of Fiction" *(Partisan Review,* Spring 1963), Murdoch has acknowledged the fact that "it plays with a philosophical idea. The problem which is mentioned in the title is the problem of how far conceptualizing and theorizing ... in fact divide you from the thing that is the object of theoretical attention." In this novel that "plays with a philosophical idea" it is significant, then, that Hugo Belfounder, whom Murdoch describes in the interview as "a sort of non-philosophical metaphysician ... paralyzed in a way by this problem" goes off at the end of the novel to become a watchmaker in acknowledgment of the twentieth century's affiliation with the world of the eighteenth century.

Still, the philosophical "idea" which is the starting point of the novel is only that—a starting point—and only in the general sense that any novel which expresses a clearly thought-about world view is "philosophical" can *Under the Net* be called a philosophical novel. It takes off in too many directions from the basic idea and evolves finally into a statement of the density and messiness of human life so that if its title comes from Wittgenstein, the novel that finally exists makes more appropriate the suggestion that Joyce, with his images and conception of nets, ought to have been the source of the title.

It is Jake, the character modeled on Beckett's Murphy and Queneau's Pierrot, who is the hero of the novel (in the sense that Nick Carroway, Jack Burden, and Marlow are the heroes, respectively, of *The Great Gatsby, All the King's Men,* and *Heart of Darkness*), for it is what Jake knows and doesn't know, the limitations of human knowledge about other people that he finally can accept, which is the real action of the novel, although in Murdoch's novel, typically, there are no epiphanies and no moments for single, significant actions which become symbolic of achieved growth. Instead, Jake and the dog are left together at the end of the novel out of necessity and choice, but hardly a choice that could qualify as a grand and gratuitous gesture. Peter Wolfe, in his fine study of Murdoch's early novels, suggesting an extensive comparison between Murdoch's novel and Joyce's work, claims that "Jake's vision at Mrs. Tinck's—the reproductive habits of her cats suggest life just as adequately as the Irish Sea—corresponds roughly to Stephen's epiphany." But if this is epiphany, like so much of Murdoch, it is ironic in its being and its statement. The fact that it follows the much more drawn-out process of Jake's realization that he must accept a world of contingency and the inability of any human being to know another, makes Jake's notion about the genetic inheritance of cats as "one of the wonders of the world," most likely a joke on all epiphany-hunters.

It is clear, given Murdoch's ideas about the novel and her admiration for the achievement of the nineteenth-century novel, why character is the most important component of her novels, but this emphasis on density of character ought to be taken within the context of the novelist's possibilities. The world out of which and in which Murdoch writes is what the twentieth century has made of it and thus it is a mistake to try to judge Murdoch's novels as if they were mere demonstrations of her critical theories and preferences. She has worked toward the idea of using more characters in the full opacity and density of their being, creating characters that could withstand the tendency of plot or myth (the influence of the crystalline) to take over at the expense of character. To write novels achieving that ideal toward which her work moves would be to falsify with a facile and dishonest idea of twentieth-century realities. Murdoch might, for example, have chosen to write historical novels in which fantasy could provide the fictional world in which to demonstrate her ideas, but to have done so would have been to abandon at the outset the truth that is the basis of her concern with character.

Murdoch's novelistic intention seems to be to try to reclaim certain possibilities for human life within the twentieth-century context, and the result of this attempt has often been the awkwardness, the mixing of elements, the warring of parts that so discomfits Murdoch's readers. A result of this intention has been as many partial failures as partial successes, but whatever judgment is finally brought to bear on Murdoch's achievement, it must acknowledge that at no point does she opt for the easy way out of what, given her view of things, has to be a dilemma which fiction cannot solve, only explore.

Within Murdoch's own literary canon, form and myth seem to war against her stated ideas about the uniqueness of the individual person and the novelist's need to give character room to develop as "substantial, impenetrable, individual, indefinable" people. Her admiration, expressed in "The Sublime and the Beautiful Revisited," for George Eliot's ability to display in her novels "that godlike capacity for so respecting and loving her characters as to make them exist as free and separate beings," reflects an admiration that some critics have withheld from Murdoch's own work, condemning her for her inability to create in fact (fiction) what she has admired in theory. An example of what happens when Murdoch's novels are judged by the example of her critical theory is found in the following:

> Miss Murdoch's enthusiasm for nineteenth-century characters prompts her desire to give "a lot of people" an existence separate from herself and to permit them to roam freely and cheerfully through her pages. Unfortunately, she seems unable to do this, for in each successive novel there

emerges a pattern of predictable and predetermined types. (Kuehl)

To speak to a need in twentieth-century fiction by way of admiring what has been lost to it is not to deny the cause of the need, is no license to falsify, which is what those critics who read Murdoch's novels as a working-out of her philosophical and critical observations seem to ask. Murdoch has herself acknowledged in several interviews her inability to prevent her characters from being overwhelmed by myth. Contingency, it would seem, is a factor even in the creation of novels about contingency, and given the background of determinism, behaviorism, and the Welfare State, against which her characters must move, the struggle to create character is an uneven and uphill battle.

Murdoch makes an attempt to draw the Welfare State and the implications of a valueless world in her second novel, *The Flight from the Enchanter* (1956), a novel in which many of the characters are aliens, displaced persons without homeland or legal existence, a state of affairs which clearly symbolizes their spiritual and psychological conditions of estrangement from the world, from each other, and from themselves. Rosa Keepe, who, without knowing it, is herself one of the dispossessed in spirit, tries to make up for the sufferings of the Lusiewicz brothers, to offer in her person an answer to their homelessness, but she can only parody the brothers' first affair with the village schoolmistress in their Polish home. She fails to see the brothers except as stereotyped outcasts, as recipients of her liberalism, and it is no surprise that, in her turn, she is only an object to them. It is in a logical extension of her attempt to alleviate their homelessness by offering her body that Jan appropriates Annette Cockeyne's jewels and Stephan moves into Rosa's house.

In *The Flight from the Enchanter,* a novel that comes down very hard on the failure of modern liberalism as essentially a failure of love, the wide and varied cast of characters and social classes demonstrates in endless ways the failure to face reality, the substitution of fantasy worlds, and the inability of individuals to reach and know others as individuals rather than as abstractions. Within the larger macrocosm of a world of political disaffection in the novel, there are numerous small, closely enforced worlds, each a failure in its own way. There are the worlds of the factory, of Hunter Keep and the *Artemis,* of Mrs. Wingfield and her crew, of Annette Cockeyne and her family, of Rainborough and SELIB, of Nina, the dressmaker, of Peter Saward and his hieroglyphics, and finally, the world that cuts across the others and seeks to draw them into a new alignment, that of the mysterious Mischa Fox and his "assistant" Calvin Blick.

Mischa Fox is the official "enchanter" of the novel, for he seems to exercise a strange power over the lives of the other characters, but in point of fact, all the characters are already enchanted by their self-deceiving views of reality. Mischa's power comes, in part, precisely because he understands the ways in which the others are self-enchanted. (One exercise of power is blackmail, and in order to carry out this particular exercise, Calvin Blick has only to photograph the other characters in their self-chosen roles.) It is Mischa Fox who replies to

Rosa's observation that the two of them look much alike: "It is an illusion of lovers." And, for all that Fox embodies neurosis, Murdoch clearly agrees.

The central problem by which Murdoch casts her characters into meaningful situations is love. In her essay on "The Sublime and the Good," the importance of love for the whole issue at stake in relation to character is made clear. "Love is the perception of individuals. Love is the extremely difficult realisation that something other than oneself is real. Love, and so art and morals, is the discovery of reality" (*Chicago Review* [Autumn 1959]). This essay, which precedes by several years the culmination of ideas in "Against Dryness," develops the same concerns that lead Murdoch toward her novelistic emphasis on character in the later, more literature-directed essay. Fantasy, in "The Sublime and the Good" is recognized as the enemy of art and of true imagination. Love, on the contrary, is an exercise of the imagination, for it involves the freeing of self from convention and fantasy, the courage to defy the tyranny of the solitary ego. "The enemies of art and of morals, the enemies that is of love are the same: social convention and neurosis."

The mind of man, of all things in nature, is the most particular and individual, and the fantasy world of the ego may prevent individuals from granting others their own reality apart from the constructed and enclosed dream world of the perceiver. Freedom, painful as it is, "is exercised in the confrontation by each other, in the context of an infinitely extensible work of imaginative understanding, of two irreducibly dissimilar individuals. Love is the imaginative recognition of, that is respect for, this otherness." In a later essay yet, ("The Darkness of Practical Reason" [*Encounter, July 1966*]), Murdoch makes a clear commitment to the idea that freedom is "to exist sanely without fear and to perceive what is real" and that "one who perceives what is real will also act rightly." Here is a nexus in which love, freedom, reality, and value come together, and because the twentieth-century world is essentially empirical, for the novelist this complexity is best expressed through character.

In the volume on Sartre, Murdoch makes clear her dislike of Virginia Woolf, whose heroine in Mrs. Dalloway, "that other lyric upon the absurdity of everything," does not, like Sartre's hero, have the good sense to feel "acute distress." The art-for-art's-sake doctrine of Bloomsbury is condemned again in "The Sublime and the Good" as a flimsy and frivolous doctrine. Art, instead, is "for life's sake, . . . or else it is worthless." This distinction is one that had been made by Murdoch in *Sartre,* in the distinction between Tolstoy and Conrad, whose writings "show forth, are nourished by, their answers to life's questions," and Proust, in whose work literature is turned into a metaphysical task, whose "work *is* his answer to life's questions."

The ability to resist the direction of Proust, the direction of Bloomsbury, is made possible in part by Murdoch's idea of the distinct value of otherness, a reality existing outside the perceiving consciousness, and her sense that this value, difficult as it may be to attain, will be grasped and practiced by the fully achieved personality. The artistic pleasures of rendering consciousness, of approximating through art the process of perception, which by definition brings the external world into the interior frame of the perceiver and thereby posits value in the act of perception itself are not sufficient for Murdoch, for there exists an implied scale of value in her view of things, for which consciousness becomes an instrument but not an absolute nor an end in itself. Thus in another context, in "The Darkness of Practical Reason," an essay reviewing the ideas in Stuart Hampshire's *Freedom of the Individual,* Murdoch insists that the mediocre man "who achieves what he intends is not the ideal of a free man," thereby implying once again the existence of a scale of values in perception and in the ability to conceive.

The action of Murdoch's novels often revolves around the *inability* to conceive possibilities, so that the apparent action of a given novel is only that conceivable to the mediocre sensibility. *The Sandcastle* (1957) is one of the clearest early examples of this kind of novel. It is clear because, despite its limited setting and socially constricted cast of characters, it is relatively open and naturalistic in its form. (Howard German, in "Allusions in the Early Novels of Iris Murdoch," a study of influences, finds something to say about Murdoch's use of sources in *The Sandcastle,* including the legend of Conary Mor, the Irish king who violates several *geise* and subsequently suffers, but if the Irish legend and other literary allusions are present in this novel, they are not necessary or operating parts of its form but rather an additional richness of detail for those readers who bring the right background to its reading.)

William Mor's is the primary consciousness of *The Sandcastle,* and his limitations are almost painful in

their ordinariness. He is indecisive, afraid of the unknown and the unpredictable, passive—all in all, the
victim of his training, of his society and its received (but
untested) standards, and of the past, his own, and the
collective notions of the past purveyed by education
and political institutions. Yet this settled, middle-aged
man is offered extraordinary opportunities, which, it is
clear, he is unable to conceive properly. He is offered
love and the practical exercise of his political beliefs,
and through both of these, the opportunity to declare
for himself the reality of a world he has pretended to
know. His failure is in part a failure of nerve, but more
important is his failure of conception. Murdoch never
says that a consummated affair with Rain Carter would
bring happiness or that election to the Labor seat in
Parliament will offer meaningful fulfillment of Mor's
social ideals. Murdoch does, in fact, present the seeds of
difficulties in both instances and the issue cannot be
reduced to the question of what William Mor has lost by
his passivity. The issue is that he has failed to face up to
the extent to which the world has offered him chances
by which to apprehend it.

The novel suggests in various ways the mean limitations of this gentle man's consciousness, and for the
reader there are hints of the novelistic ways in which
Murdoch is going in the future to pursue the difficulties
of rendering her theme. The mysterious gypsy woodcut-
ter, who appears first on the day that Mor and Rain
Carter drive into the country together, again on the
night that Rain comes to Mor's house and he fails to
become her lover, and finally on the day of Rain's
departure from Mor's life, seems to hint at the irra-

tional, to symbolize the unrealized life outside convention. And both of Mor's children, who have watched the
failures of the good, middle-class life, try to reach
outside it; Felicity with her self-defeating magic rituals
and psychic exercises and Donald with his potentially
fatal climb of the forbidden tower. While Felicity's
magical rites and her attempts to explore an alternative
reality may be the more interesting in terms of future
Murdoch novels, Donald's climbing of the tower seems
for this novel the more appropriate of the two children's
attempts to confront reality, for in it is the instrument
to destroy society's unhappy and enforced regimen over
his life and to try to shock into reality his muddled and
castrated father. (Murdoch often uses Freudian symbols
ironically as examples of the ways in which too rigid a
conception may be placed on human complexity, but
the tower in *The Sandcastle* is not ironic.) It is not
accidental that Mor's response to the action into which
he is forced is to lose consciousness. *The Sandcastle*
ends with the irony of Mor's being trapped into a role
which once would have meant freedom if he had been
able to conceive it for himself.

The problem of freedom and reality is explored again
in Murdoch's next novel, *The Bell* (1958), a novel that is
a good deal more complex than *The Sandcastle*,
although it is a novel about an attempt to acknowledge
and create an artificial social order, which is beautiful in
its simplicity, moral in its intentions, religious in its
apprehensions, self-sustaining and self-enforced. *The
Bell* has been considered one of the Murdoch's most
ambitious novels by many readers, and whether or not it
is one of the best, its totality of conception and

execution makes it one of the major works of her canon. (One of the many curious facts about Iris Murdoch as a novelist is that she seems never to have had an "apprentice" period, beginning as she does with a major and quite polished novel in *Under the Net* and proceeding to experiment with novels of different kinds, not fumbling noticeably until perhaps her eighth novel [*The Italian Girl*] — a quite remarkable achievement.)

Quite as artificial as the lay religious community at Imber Court are its ideas of morality and its notion of human personality. The community is made up of a group of people withdrawing, for various reasons, from society—trying to create an order in which, through simplicity and devotion, they may escape the complexity and randomness of the outside world. Quite predictably what they do achieve is an intensification of the problems which they have brought with them, for their artificially conceived order, failing in the same ways as the disorder of the larger society, only throws into violent relief the problems they seek to escape. The rules by which the community attempts to nourish a higher life are much too shallow to take into account the complexities of the human personality, much too narrow to contain or even conceive the infinite varieties of love. The ideas of order which are examined range from the conventional, authoritarian ideas of James Tayper Pace, the organizer of the community, to those of the wise Abbess of the cloister, which the Imber Court adjoins, who differs from Pace in her compassion and her understanding of the limits of human endeavors. It is the Abbess who tells Michael Meade, troubled by his homosexuality, that "all our failures are ultimately failures in love. Imperfect love must not be condemned and rejected, but made perfect. The way is always forward, never back." (This last, sounding like Krishna's advice, is one of the many echoes of the work of the "dry" poet of *The Four Quartets.*)

The bell referred to by the title is inscribed *"Vox ego sum amoris. Gabriel vocor,"* and it is appropriately named *Gabriel,* for the call to love in all its guises is the sound of the last trump for some of the characters (Nick and Catherine Fawley, Michael Meade, Paul Greenfield) and for others the message of new beginnings (Toby Gashe, Dora Greenfield). Murdoch does, in *The Bell,* move in the direction of opening up her novel, of admitting a large cast of characters who are given the chance to develop against a background which is rich and particular. And *The Bell* seems to be, like *The Sandcastle,* one of Murdoch's novels in which plot or fable does not fight against the development of character. It is interesting in this respect that Murdoch has to create, through the strategy of the lay religious community, a background for her characters which is artificial by design, and although the novel says clearly that because the design is too narrow it encourages neurosis, nonetheless her characters develop more freely than they do in the London novels, in which the pressure of modern society, the absence of a defining background is so strongly felt.

As in the first novel, *Under the Net,* so in *A Severed Head* do the characters yield before the force of the fable. In her interview with Kermode, Murdoch admits that *A Severed Head* "probably represents a giving in to the myth." *Which* specific myth is another question.

(Murdoch generally uses the term *myth* to mean *fable*.)
Certainly the Freudian myth of Medusa, as the castrated
and castrating woman, is there, as is the substitution of
the psychoanalyst for God in the modern world and of
his conclusions for values. The specific mythical references in the novel are many and range from classical
Greek and Oriental allusions to Freud and Jung, from
Dionysian to Christian mythology. Various critics have
exercised their ingenuity on the endless possibilities that
Murdoch has provided in this respect, but a suggestion
of special interest to the readers of this series is that of
Alice P. Kenney in her article "The Mythic History of *A
Severed Head" (Modern Fiction Studies* [Autumn
1969]), for she finds the pagan Celtic ritual of severed
heads behind Murdoch's intentions (Honor Klein is,
after all, an anthropologist), and makes a specific
connection between Honor Klein and a Celtic divinity
named Medb.

Martin Lynch-Gibbon, the man who is composing his
memoir, is, as he tells the reader, Anglo-Irish and Welsh,
and this fact may point toward the Celtic sources. At
any rate, Martin Lynch-Gibbon, an amateur historian,
admires the eighteenth century, that century Murdoch
has linked with the twentieth, and there is something of
the Restoration comedy of manners behind the form of
the novel. The characters of this novel are probably
more indulgently self-conscious than any other set of
characters assembled in the modern novel, and their
solipsistic frenzy is encouraged by modern psychiatry,
which seeks to give it form and meaning. The self-con-
sciously enlightened bed-hopping of the novel brings the
narrator of the novel and Honor Klein together by the

end of the book, both wiser for their experiences and ready, perhaps, if the final page is any indication, to accept the contingency of life without the kind of crippling self-dramatizing that has provided the action of the novel.

An Unofficial Rose (1962) is, like *The Sandcastle,* a domestic novel, as are *The Nice and the Good* (1968), *A Fairly Honourable Defeat* (1970), and *An Accidental Man* (1971). No single term can adequately cover the variety which Murdoch is able to bring to a given novelistic approach, but this group of novels is one in which the family unit and its relationships form a center from which to examine the complex question of love. (This distinction is a difficult one to make since *The Italian Girl, Bruno's Dream,* and *The Time of the Angels* are novels built around family relationships, but the central concerns are elsewhere than in what can be revealed of human limitations and triumphs in the casual give and take of daily alignments.) And although parts of each of these novels take place in the city, representative of the impersonal force of modern life, the background of each is more tradional, inhabited, reciprocal than those of *Under the Net* or *A Severed Head. An Unofficial Rose,* for example, takes place mostly at two country estates with long-established traditions including the cultivation of exotic roses. Within this setting, however, the characters rebel against the gentility which stifles them, but their rebellion involves the flight into romantic fantasy, which only separates them from reality. Yet the characters in this novel are spread out, well developed by their author even in their failings, and the failures of the characters make clear that flight from the present does not guarantee freedom and that fantasy can never lead to freedom. Thus Hugh Peronett and his son pursue Emma Sands and Lindsay Rimmer because of a failure of imagination, a failure of the "imaginative recognition of . . . otherness," which Murdoch has diagnosed as the necessary definition of love, about which Hugh learns something at the end of the novel.

Classifying *The Nice and the Good* as a domestic novel calls for a qualification, for there are in this novel the elements of dark powers: occultism, blackmail, murder, suicide, sexual scandals. However, the material of this dark world of London is played off against a quite ordinary summer holiday by the sea at Trescombe. John Duncane, the character who mediates between the two worlds, is set the task of investigating the underground world of the suicide, but he discovers his true task to be an investigation of his own moral values and an acceptance of Mary Clothier, the epitome of the "good." The extent of his change is symbolized by his being trapped in the underwater cave with Pierce, Mary's troubled adolescent son, where they huddle together like twin fetuses, and John comes to the knowledge that "To love and to reconcile and to forgive, only this matters. All power is sin and all law is frailty. Love is the only justice. Forgiveness, reconciliation, not law." As he and Pierce swim out of the the opening of the cave after the tide recedes, it is Mary Clothier who puts her coat around his naked body, and he is now ready to make one half of one of the couples by whose joining Murdoch says so much about the human condition, judging by the ability of separate people to most accept themselves as they acknowledge the individuality of others.

Even though, as Frank Baldanza puts it (*Modern Fiction Studies* [Autumn 1969]), the theme of this novel is the exorcising of demons, many of the demons belong to the ordinary world of sunlight and sea, and they are demons growing out of failed relationships and the inability to master the past. Yet these demons belong to the characters who, as Rubin Rabinovitz suggests (*Iris Murdoch* 1968), "conform to the 'ordinary morality' of the linguistic analysts; they are kind, cheerful, happy, and benignly unaware that beyond their niceness is an ethical level more nearly perfect and more painfully achieved."

The same kind of openness which allows character to develop is present in the other domestic novels, although in some ways, *A Fairly Honourable Defeat* moves back toward the comedy of manners of *A Severed Head,* once again demonstrating the difficulty of categorizing Murdoch's fictional creations. (It does take place in London, although in part in a suburban setting complete with garden and swimming pool.) The role of Palmer Anderson, the god-substitute psychoanalyst, is taken in the later novel by Julius King, whose Jewish parents have Christianized his name from Kahn, so that he is ironically, by name at least, emperor and king. He is, once again, a scientist, but not of that "muddled, embryonic science" Murdoch judges psychoanalysis to be.

Julius King, who himself survived the Nazi concentration camps, has worked on biological warfare projects before the action of the novel begins. He carries his

scientific attitude over into the world of real people and
tries to demonstrate "the frailty of human attach-
ments." He discovers, however, that he cannot control
the contingent, and although he proves in part his
theory that people can be manipulated because of their
own romantic and self-consuming views of reality, he
cannot control the consequences of his actions nor, in
the event that love operates as a "recognition of
otherness," can he succeed. Axel and Simon, the
homosexual couple, manage to survive Julius's manipulations as they learn to respect each other's separateness,
and the novel ends with the two juxtaposed scenes of
Axel and Simon together in the south of France and
Julius alone in Paris. In the last chapter, which belongs
to Julius, he is alone by choice and full of a sense of
well-being; there is no remorse, and he is aware of
himself in a totally self-centered way. The suffering of
the others has not touched him; he is entirely separate
from it, even thriving on it. As the novel ends he is
preparing to enjoy a meal at a restaurant recommended
to him by Rupert, the man he has killed by his
manipulations. The last chapter of *A Fairly Honourable
Defeat* suggests that Murdoch has written again *The
Flight from the Enchanter* (even Tollis and his concern
with educating the working classes echoes the earlier
novel) but with less frenzy and distortion, the man of
science replacing the man of mysterious international
intrigue—altogether a more convincing rendering of
modern malaise.

An Accidental Man moves further away from plot or
fable than any of Murdoch's previous works, and it
reaches toward the outside limits of the domestic novel

of manners. The egoistic characters do violence on one another in their relationships, never arriving at much that could pass as self-knowledge, with the limited exceptions of Matthew, Charlotte, and Ludwig—all characters who leave the society of London and go their various ways, each conscious of the partially unsatisfactory possibilities before him.

An Accidental Man tries through several stylistic devices to underwrite the shallowness of modern society as it is conceived by its characters. The novel is, in part, epistolary, with conflicting views of reality arriving via the notations of the socially witty letter, which serves little in the cause of communication but a good deal more by way of revealing each writer's preoccupations. (The letter has been a device used in earlier novels to state the inability of various characters to conceive the externality of the world, for often several versions of reality are written out in unsent letters, fabricated and rearranged as if they existed only in the formality of their expression.) And the novel ends with a long exchange of party conversation, social gossip which conveys information of sorts (within the same limitations as the letters), in which people are reduced to one-line effects. The novel's last lines are the *good nights* echoing the end of "A Game of Chess" in *The Waste Land.*

In *The Nice and the Good,* a novel with its own Shakespearean echoes, one of the characters asks why Shakespeare didn't write about Merlin, or, another asks, about the Arthurian legends. The answer, which comes from Mary Clothier, is halting and tentative, failing to express what she *knows* about the largeness of Shakespeare's world: "Shakespeare knew . . . that world of magic . . . the subject was dangerous . . . and those sort of relationships . . . not quite in the real world . . . it just wasn't his sort of thing . . . and it had such a definite atmosphere of its own . . . he just couldn't use it . . . ." Murdoch herself has ventured into that world of magic and medieval myth, and, to an extent, what she says of Shakespeare comments on the luck of her own novelistic encounters.

In *The Unicorn* (1963), *The Italian Girl* (1964), *The Time of the Angels* (1966), and *Bruno's Dream* (1969), Murdoch moves into a darker world in which the boundaries of a naturalistic reality may be momentarily brushed aside, but the central concerns of the other novels are not changed. The theme of power and the ways in which victims deliver themselves up is present in all these novels as is Murdoch's ever-present examination of the possible ways man can define his human possibilities through love.

The Unicorn, which is influenced by the work of the Irish writer of gothic tales, Sheridan LeFanu, is probably the best of these four novels, although *Bruno's Dream* is perhaps the most interesting. *The Unicorn,* which is unabashedly gothic, takes place against the background of a world at once artificial and natural, a world in which the various characters' *ideas* about reality create a necessity by which they live. The cooperative setting— with its treacherous and rocky sea coast, its forbidding and sterile land, its dangerous bogs—is dominated by two isolated country houses in which the local gentry act out agreed-upon roles whose limits and prescriptions have taken on the force of sanctions or taboos.

According to A. S. Byatt (*Degrees of Freedom* 1965), the unspecified setting of the novel resembles Ireland, and the reader is meant to sense in the story the kind of guilt identified by V. S. Pritchett as being implicit in Anglo-Irish society and behind the successful ghost stories of LeFanu. Perhaps Murdoch's acknowledgment of LeFanu as a source invites the Irish relationship, but the persistent identification of the world of the novel with *Wuthering Heights* or with the novels of Thomas Hardy by other critics, suggests that for Murdoch's purposes the unspecified, nonlocalized scene better serves her purposes. Robert Scholes in *The Fabulators* chooses *The Unicorn* as his example of modern allegorical fabulation, and the movement toward allegory in the novel is a move away from precise localization, although the setting, wherever it is, does provide that kind of specification and detail against which Murdoch's characters develop best, although they are, in the "dark" novels, in as much danger of being overwhelmed by background as the characters are in the London novels of being underwhelmed, of not being identifiable because of the colorless modern mechanized world in which they exist.

It is difficult to begin to touch on the possibilities of this novel, which seems to offer the most successfully created and balanced density of relationships between plot, character and symbolic meanings of Murdoch's gothic forays. Hannah Crean-Smith is the unattainable center around whom the other characters revolve and define themselves. She was, according to Murdoch ("An Interview with Iris Murdoch," *University of Windsor Review* [Spring 1965]), intended to be a kind of Christ figure, "a saviour who would expiate the sins of those about her through suffering," who became unsuitable as "an image of redemption." Hannah is the sacrificial scapegoat in that she is the figure created and possessed by others, thereby giving meaning to their lives, although she ultimately is substantial enought to be forced into several acts of violence which contradict her trancelike, passive state of much of the novel—the state in which she is being defined by others. Hannah Crean-Smith, whose names are both palindromatic and anagrammatic by way of suggesting the mystery at the core of her being, is seen and desired by those outside her (hers is the one major character defined entirely from without except as her two final actions have a life of their own). She is the center for the characters from the Riders household, a representation of the Classical (artistic and philosophical) virtues, and for those from Gaze, representing feudal Christianity, and for those two from the outside world, Marian and Effingham—the two who survive the wreckage of the fantasy world to return to the "real" world. Hannah is, to use Murdoch's, term, not accorded "otherness" by the characters of the novel. She is the unicorn which, like Hannah, exists only in the fantasy of those who find a vacuum in the world because they cannot see its real substance.

Both Effingham and Marian come from the world outside Gaze (the feudal house whose name suggests the solipsistic, self-frozen stare of Yeats's moon-struck heron of *Calvary*) and as a result of their experiences return to it with a greater understanding of themselves and their relationship to the world. Effingham, whose devotion to Hannah has been to the *idea* of the suffering, imprisoned lady, is forced by circumstances into attempting a rescue of her which is foredoomed to be destructive on every level, including that of his conceptual world, and having destroyed the tenuous balance of their relationship, having violated the *idea* of the courtly figure of Hannah awaiting rescue, he wanders off into the bog in which he loses his way and, facing death, experiences a knowing relationship to existence which is like that of Ducane's as he faces death by water in *The Nice and the Good.*

These moments of real knowledge are, I suppose, the epiphanies Murdoch offers her readers, but they are not abstract, symbolic, or transcendent; they are instead a conscious formulation of what the characters have been learning about experience—a facing of that which has been avoided through the operation of fantasy. What Effingham realizes as he loses his obscuring sense of self before the almost certain approach of death is that "What was left was everything else, all that was not himself, that object which he had never before seen and upon which he now gazed with the passion of a lover. And indeed he could always have known this, for the fact of death stretches the length of life. . . . with the death of the self the world becomes quite automatically the object of perfect love."

Marian attains her freedom by her final willingness to accept the separateness of others. It is she who realizes that Denis (the keeper of the fish) is "becoming Hannah, now," a real Christ-scapegoat, who takes on himself the guilt of the others and fulfills Max Le Jour's idea of Ate: the almost automatic transfer of suffering from one being to another. She is able to let go of Denis and return "to the real world. She would dance at Geoffrey's wedding."

The Italian Girl and *The Time of the Angels* are the two weakest novels in the Murdoch canon, novels in which Murdoch's characters and moral points of view are overwhelmed by the machinery of darkness. In *The Italian Girl* (which Wolfe in *The Disciplined Heart* sees as influenced by Murdoch's work with J. B. Priestly on the stage version of *A Severed Head*) the major character, Edmund Narraway, suffers from an Oedipus complex, as does Martin Lynch-Gibbon of the earlier novel, and the solution is much the same. But in *A Severed Head,* Lynch-Gibbon does not have to make his way through dark old houses, dark passions, melodramatic fires, and a mother and daughter both made pregnant by the same enigmatic Russian Jew. On the contrary, *A Severed Head* moves with some good humor, irony, and urbanity as a comedy of manners whereas *The Italian Girl* cannot survive the weight of the collapsing Narraway house. The chapter titles for *The Italian Girl* suggest that Murdoch's purpose is ironic, but her people, failing once again because of their self-enclosing fantasies, are not substantial enough to bear the light of the real world, even that of the Eternal City.

The Time of the Angels has many of the same problems as *The Italian Girl,* although its examination of religious consequences provides a center lacking in the earlier novel. The novel counterpoints two worlds, that of the inhabitants of the rectory and that of the "normal," socially oriented professionals: the schoolmaster, Marcus, who is himself at work on a book probably to be called *Morality in a World without God;* the humanist-busybody, Norah Shadox-Brown; the Anglican bishop; and, finally, Anthea Barlow, ex-wife turned psychiatric social worker.

The rectory, which is in some ways more interesting than the characters that inhabit it, is quite appropriately not attached to a church; the church to which it belonged had been bombed to rubble during the war. The rectory, a totally enclosed fortress against the outside world, is the dark home of Carel, an Anglican priest, who worships not God but Satan. God is dead, His death releasing the angels of darkness, angels best served in the exercise of power. Below the rectory runs an underground railway that rumbles in its subterranean depths. Its lower level belongs to the servants, the unknowable East European refugees common to Murdoch's novels, and a Black-Irish servant girl, who is one of the rector's mistresses. On the floors above, besides the rector, there are the two girls, one languishing with a mysterious illness. Incest is only one of the ways in which Carel mocks his vows as well as in the corruption of the young. Carel is not able to fill the void left by the death of God, and his suicide is the most logical action of this melodramatic novel.

In *Bruno's Dream* Murdoch comes closer to finding a more successful balance for her novel, although *Bruno's Dream* has troubled her critics more than any of her other major novels, in part because their instinct to consider it a serious work appears to be countered by the novelist's playfulness in its conclusion, in part because of the mixed moods involved, and in part because Murdoch seems perversely to have given her most cherished moral ideas to the most troublesome of the characters. She has, in short, forced the readers of this novel to perform that difficult action she asks of her characters who are to progress; she asks that her readers accept a contingency within the fictional convention that challenges their expectations.

Bruno's Dream centers around the lingering death of an old man, helpless and physically revolting, who in dying has come to resemble the spiders which inhabit his old mansion and have provided him in the past with an amateur scientific interest. The novel is filled with the ever-present, if shifting, Murdoch couples. For Miles, Bruno's estranged son, there are three women: Parvati, his dead Indian wife; Diana, his present wife, and Lisa, whom he loves. For Danby, the dandy son-in-law who cares for Bruno, there is again a dead woman, his wife who killed herself; Adelaide the maid below the stairs, and Lisa, with whom Danby ends in perfect bliss despite the fact that she has taken up with him perhaps because she wishes to torture Miles or because she honors Miles's marriage to her sister Diana. Bruno's dying consciousness is the scene of an ongoing warfare between his dead wife, Janie, and Maureen, his Liverpool-Irish mistress. In addition there are the servants, Will, who loves Adelaide, and Nigel, who loves Danby, and Adelaide, who loves Danby and Will.

Given the possibilities inherent in such a cast of characters, Murdoch finds plenty of takers for the often outrageous actions of the novel, such as the duel between Danby and Will Boase over the honor of Adelaide the Maid. The outrageous and the macabre elements of the novel are treated alike with a comic

touch, in both cases made possible by the solipsism of the characters. For example, Miles, who fancies himself a poet, has transformed the death of Parvati into an occasion for poetry. He has bent his fancy upon it, and it is not until many years later that he faces her death as a fact rather than seeing it as an art object which he has created.

The ubiquitous Nigel, one of the strangest characters in a strange novel, is Bruno's male nurse and twin to the thief and blackmailer Will Boase. Nigel is a practitioner of Hindu mysticism and a source of a good deal of the book's wisdom. In a letter he writes to Danby he describes the situation of love as it exists so often in Murdoch's novels:

> the worthless can love the good, the good the worthless, the worthless the worthless and the good the good. Hey presto: and the great light flashes on revealing perhaps reality or perhaps illusion. And alas how very often, dearest Danby, does one love alone, in solipsism, in vain incapsulation. . . . It is not a matter of conventions. Love knows no conventions. Anything *can* happen, so that in a way, a terrible terrible way, there are no impossibilities.

It is also Nigel who gives Diana the wisdom she needs to accept her condition at the end of the novel. Nigel, claiming to be God (". . . it can be that I am the false god, or one of the million million false gods there are. It matters very little. The false god is the true God. Up any religion a man may climb."), tells her to forgive Miles and Lisa: "Let them trample over you in their own way." In the renunciation Miles and Lisa have made, Nigel quite rightly denies them an element of sacrifice and sees that "each loves himself. . . . They have sacrificed nothing. They have just decided to do what will make them flourish." Nigel sounds a good deal like Murdoch when he tells Diana that "A human being hardly ever thinks about other people. He contemplates fantasms which resemble them and which he has decked out for his own purposes."

Miles the man who makes such a self-conscious effort as a poet to *see*, is the perfect example of Nigel's commentary. When Miles falls in love with Lisa, he realizes that he had never really seen her in the past because he had looked at her only through Diana's stereotyping of her as "the bird with a broken wing," and yet when he feels he can see her as a separate person in touch with the hard reality of the poor, he mistakes the truth once again. Finally, when he has to confront the image of Lisa and Danby happily consoling themselves with each other, his own self-enclosing views of her are taxed to the limits of endurance.

The novel ends with expectations turned upside down. Nigel goes off to work in the Save the Children Federation, taking Lisa's place. Lisa, the self-proclaimed, self-sacrificing, failed nun, as Danby's consort, having convinced him that (as every Murdoch reader knows by now) "Romantic love is not an absolute," takes the place both Nigel and Diana have longed for. Miles has his muse and sits, literally encapsulated and separate, in his summer house, while Diana, who has begun to resemble Lisa as she used to be, loves the dying Bruno in spite of herself and lives his death, knowing with Nigel's help that love "was the only thing that existed."

Strangest of all is the Victorian transformation

reported for the future lives of Will Boase and his new wife, Adelaide, whose twin sons, Mercutio and Benedick, will go to Oxford after their parents have become Lord and Lady Boase, Will having become one of the most famous Shakespearean actors in England. It is as if the flooding Thames, which inundated Bruno's house, had left behind a world as different as that left after the Biblical flood of forty days and forty nights.

It is no wonder that readers and critics are thrown off balance by this novel Murdoch has created. There is, for almost every character in the novel, a point at which he could have suffered death or violence and yet does not, but lives on (with the exception of Nigel, Diana, and Bruno) unchanged in greatly changed circumstances. In short, the comic mode prevails.

Murdoch has, in *Bruno's Dream,* come close to a successful joining of domestic comedy and macabre elements and, at the same time, to the successful creation of a novel in which characters could develop without being overwhelmed by the machinery necessary to realign the reader's apprehension of the world. She has here used form, that "great consolation of love" and "also its great temptation," in such an exaggerated way that the otherness of the characters and of the world has been forced upon the reader (notice that Nigel has physically to force his hearers into attention). By exploiting the unpredictable and irrational, Murdoch has once again denied the absolute limits of a rationalistic, human-centered universe.

At this stage of assessing Murdoch's achievement as a novelist, the appropriate question is not whether the new novel, *The Black Prince,* or any of its successors will be failures or successes but whether or not her courage and ingenuity can survive the difficulties attendant upon writing with her preoccupations in a world bent quite otherwise and bring a sufficient audience of readers to that state of "loving attention" which is the only possible way to apprehend the world.

2

The Red and the Green

If the "Irish" novel is obligatory for the novelist born in Ireland, then *The Red and the Green* must stand in this relationship to the career of Iris Murdoch, for it is a novel that takes Ireland as its subject—a subject approached with a good deal of self-conscious ambivalence. It is a novel written as if Murdoch had set out to explore the "Irish Question" without hope of an "Irish Answer," and it is not without significance that the *Epilogue* takes place in England in 1938, achieving physically the distance felt throughout the novel. In *The Red and the Green,* Ireland and the Easter Rising provide the subject matter, as they do for Yeats's poem, "Easter 1916," but the feeling and the involvement Yeats embodies in the poem are never achieved in the novel. This is not to suggest that Yeats's attitudes toward the Rising were less ambivalent or complexly critical than Murdoch's. It is simply that in Murdoch's novel there is an academic thoroughness, which in its determination to view the subject from every possible facet, results in a distancing from the subject that makes it forever *object.*

Still it is necessary to qualify one's agreement with Rubin Rabinovitz that "Despite a certain amount of talk about Irish politics, the historical setting is not of prime importance in *The Red and the Green*; with a few changes in background the novel could have been set in the time of the American Civil War, or the Bolshevik Revolution." The thrust of Rabinovitz's comment is clear: the Rising, which preceded by several years the birth of Jean Iris Murdoch in Dublin, provides a historical setting and an occasion for the novel which never achieves the sense of inevitability that setting attains in fully realized fiction. It is as hard to imagine *Moby Dick* without the sea as it is to conceptualize *Heart of Darkness* set in any other part of the world than Africa, but in *The Red and the Green,* the setting, while not quite incidental, is too often coincidental. Bloom will forever wander through the Dublin streets, but his ersatz cousin, Barnaby Drumm, could suffer relocation without absolute violence.

The failure of setting in *The Red and the Green* grows not, I think, as Rabinovitz suggests, from its accidental nature, its easy interchangeability, but rather from the distance with which it is treated by Murdoch. In this novel, the Rising and the Irish are something which one has opinions *about,* and, apparently, the more varied the expression of opinions, the more truthful the novel tries to be. Although this is an equation which has worked for Murdoch before (in *A Severed Head, The Bell,* and others), there are certain emotional responses inherent in the Irish situation which militate against the formula of meaning through objective multiplicity.

Murdoch is quite *serious,* in a philosophical and literary sense, about her material in this novel, lacking only the seriousness of feeling, without which even the best novel about Ireland becomes a "colonial" novel. Joyce is a good case in point here, for although his attitudes about Ireland are never simple, and often contradictory, the commitment to feeling is never in doubt. The same is true of Yeats in "Easter 1916," a poem in which Yeats is much given to polemic and yet in which private feeling enters commensurate to if not consonant with the public feeling inherent in the situation.

Perhaps it is unfair to compare a short poem and a novel, and yet the novel Murdoch has written seems to mirror Yeats's poem in its general form, beginning as it does with the assembling of the local cast of characters of the (not always) "casual comedy" and running through the roll, as does Yeats, of those more public characters who are to take their parts in the transformation of sacrifice. Not only do both novel and poem work with the same materials, the questions they ask about the objective meaning of sacrifice, the terrible personal cost ("Too long a sacrifice/Can make a stone of the heart."), the political necessities of the insurrection, and the transfiguration of myth are the same. And more, a good deal of the local texture of both works is similar. Murdoch picks up, for example, the general ambience and meaning of horse and horseman, symbols which occur throughout Yeats's work to suggest moral aristocracy, freedom, daring, and mastery, and which are invoked specifically in "Easter 1916" in the naming of Constance Marciewicz, in the image of the winged horse of Padraic Pearse, and in the natural image of the living horse and rider set against the stone in the midst of the stream.

In *The Red and the Green,* Murdoch sets up, by measure of their horsemanship, an easy distance between Andrew Chase-White, Anglo-Irish by family but apparently English by inclination, and his Irish cousins. Second Lieutenant Andrew Chase-White, the only regularly commissioned soldier of the novel, wears the uniform of King Edward's Horse, but he fears and detests horses. The motivation for his unlikely enlistment is fairly simple. His childhood has been blighted by his inability to compete successfully with his Irish cousins: "This had especially been so in the matter of horses. All his cousins were natural, casual riders. They were a race of young horsemen, passing him by with the insolence of the mounted." (In case the general reference does not point clearly enough to the Yeatsian "horseman" and all it implies, Murdoch through syntactical rearrangement invokes the final lines of "Under Ben Bulben": "Horseman, pass by!") Even Frances, Andrew's intended, is described so that the reader knows her spiritual ancestors to be the Sidhe of Irish mythology: "Frances, who was herself a remote relation and had belonged to the 'gang,' [was] . . . a swift mounted girl, a graceful side-saddle Amazon, outdistancing him, disappearing." Millie, who, in part, suggests Countess Marciewicz, is identified with the savage and beautiful hunters she owns as is the only man worthy of her, Andrew's oldest cousin, Pat Dumay. (The reader should not be quite so surprised as he is at the end of

the novel to learn that all the time it is Pat Dumay that
Frances has loved, for no Irish horsewoman could settle
for less.)

In the epilogue, the novel asks the same question as
Yeats's poem, "Was it needless death after all?" and the
answer, if one is to accept Frances's experience of the
event, is the same as Yeats's conclusion that it is
". . . enough/to know they dreamed and are dead."
Murdoch, like Yeats, intones the magic names: "Pearse,
Connolly, MacDonagh, MacDermott, MacBride, Joseph
Plunkett—And they hanged Roger Casement," and
through Frances, also acknowledges that "a terrible
beauty is born."

> They, those others, had a beauty which could not be
> eclipsed or rivalled. They had been made young and perfect
> forever, safe from the corruption of time and from those
> ambiguous second thoughts which dim the brightest face of
> youth. In the undivided strength of their first loves they
> had died, and their mothers had wept for them, and had it
> been for nothing? Because of their perfection she could not
> bring herself to say so. They had died for glorious things,
> for justice, for freedom, for Ireland.

The problem with giving the concluding voice of the
novel to Frances is that the role falls to her simply
because she is, as she says, a "survivor." She is an
Ishmael stepping forth to speak to us from the vortex,
and it is precisely here that one of the difficulties with
the epilogue (and hence the novel) is underlined, for
there is nothing inherent in the novel or in the character
of Frances that makes the weight of final judgment that
falls on her either appropriate or inevitable. Murdoch
has, at the eleventh hour, tried to give the weight of
feeling to her exploration of the red and the green, but

it comes as a jarring note to a novel that has so carefully argued all the sides and all the possible meanings of Irish history.

If Murdoch did, consciously or not, call on Yeats's poem as a model of sorts, then it is at the point of conclusion that she is led to take her novel where it cannot go. In the poem, the single speaker, denied participation in the event itself, can make his own gesture in full awareness of its ambiguities. He writes out in a verse the names of those who have died, taking all their bewilderment and artificially simplifying it into the color of their politics. With the same singleness of purpose that the dead suffered, the poet, both setting aside and exercising the complexity he knows, writes, "Wherever green is worn," and makes within his poem a place for a consciously reductive "Irish" verse without denying the complexity of the whole. The Irish dead have earned his obligatory verse, and he, by his acceptance of his role as Irish rhymer, by his action, takes his place at their side. The verse which concludes the poem does not, however, deny the unreconciled complexity of that which has gone before, and it is the mark of Yeats's high achievement that the final line of the commemorative verse still retains the ambiguous and difficult knowledge that belongs to the *persona* of the poem: "A terrible beauty is born."

Thus Yeats's poem achieves a kind of wholeness by virtue of its coda which simply cannot be imitated by the epilogue of the Murdoch novel. The final scene of the Rising in *The Red and the Green* much better epitomizes the novel, for in it the reader is left with the image of Andrew Chase-White, the uniformed British officer, handcuffed to Cathal Dumay, hearing the confused and often hostile voices of the inhabitants of Dublin after the Easter Rising, and this is an image and an echo which underwrites the complexities and imperfections of human actions, motives, and history. Perhaps the epilogue means to suggest that only in memory transformed by human emotion is beauty given, are the young "made perfect forever," but because the memory seems gratuitously given to Frances, and because the book has examined, among other things, the destructive potential of romantic self-deception, the reader experiences difficulty with the epilogue in the context of the whole. Perhaps the epilogue as a gesture of feeling, as an imaginative statement of faith, is the most "Irish" thing in the book, but it seems as uncomfortably joined to the novel as Cathal Dumay manacled to Andrew Chase-White on that long-awaited day.

More typical than the epilogue is the general desire of the novelist to hold opposing views of Ireland in evidence. This desire results in the educational symposia which seem to take place whenever Ireland is the topic of conversation. Frances takes part in many of these, and there is nothing to presage the feelings ascribed to her in the final section. For example, early in the novel, Frances's father, Christopher Bellman, who later is to die trying to join the rebels in the Post Office, brings a report of a cheering crowd at an assembly of the Irish Citizens Army with bugles and banners:

> "But what did it mean?" said Andrew.
> "Nothing. That's my point. The Irish are so used to personifying Ireland as a tragic female, any patriotic stimulus produces an overflow of sentiment at once."

" 'Did you see an old woman going down the path?' 'I
did not, but I saw a young girl, and she had the walk of a
queen.' "

"Precisely, Frances. Saint Teresa's Hall nearly fell down
when Yeats first came out with that stuff. Though, in fact,
if you recited the Dublin telephone directory in this town
with enough feeling you'd have people shedding tears."

That the novel proper is full of complexity is
suggested by its title, which critics who do bother to
deal with this novel read much too one-dimensionally.
Typical of the general assumption is the statement of
Peter Kemp ("The Fight Against Fantasy: Iris Mur-
doch's *The Red and the Green*" [*Modern Fiction
Studies,* Autumn 1969]) that the "red" and the
"green" are "the opposing English and Irish forces."
Kemp finds support for his reading in the song that
Cathal sings:

> Sure 'twas for this Lord Edward died
> and Wolfe Tone sunk serene,
> Because they could not bear to leave
> the red above the green.

The opposition of the English and the Irish is everywhere in the novel—historical, political, religious,
temperamental, economic. It is the subject of much
discussion, action, and emotion, and yet finally, with a
few exceptions it is, to a large extent, as Rabinovitz
suggests with some justice, the frame upon which the
novel is hung.

If the novel succeeds, its accomplishment is not in
politics but in character, and it is here that the title is
also suggestive in ways not seen by a critic like Kemp,
who is willing to read the title only on its simplest level
and hence tends to see the novel as being concerned

"not so much with people and their relationships, as with a central theme, the characters being chosen to illustrate this and their movements determined by its dictates. In place of contingency, necessity has been imposed." Strangely enough, it is just in that failure to find in necessity, in an external pattern and its demands, the meanings that they seek that the characters in this novel take their places in the canon of Iris Murdoch's work. The *green* of the title are not all Irish even, for in the sense that all the characters fail of ripeness, lack the experiences which they hunger after, mistake dreams of action for meaning, they do not ever find in their own relationships to the pattern the justice they seek. If ripeness is all, it would be a strange turn for Murdoch to confer it automatically upon her Irish characters because of their relationship even to an idea that led to the seizing of the Post Office in Dublin. Rather, it is in their own tendencies to see the world in the noncontingent terms of red and green, English and Irish, that the characters are marked as "green."

The reader recalls, in this context, Frances's questions about the meaning of the agony of patriotism about to befall Ireland. "What," she asks, "will Home Rule do for that woman begging in the streets?" And she concludes that she herself wouldn't know which uniform to wear, even in the Great War against Germany, shocking her auditor by her further assertion that if Andrew were to become a conscientious objector, she would "fall down and worship him." It is perhaps this exchange and others like it that make Frances so surprising in her role as the final voice of the novel which is the source of praise for the accomplishment of the Easter Rising. Although it is possible that in her commitment to the

Rising is meant to be the literal evidence that, by the act
of sacrifice, "all is changed, changed utterly."

If the title is to be torn away from its more obvious
political intentions, the *red* clearly speaks to the idea of
sacrifice, the blood of the Easter Rising as well as that
being shed in the larger war in France, a war of which
the reader is continually reminded. At the end of the
novel, it is made clear by the references to the Civil War
in Ireland and the war in Spain that there is no end to
the blood sacrifice demanded of individuals. There are
hints that Frances's tall son, who talks like Cathal
Dumay, will perhaps be going to Spain before that war
is done, and the circle will continue.

The red of sacrifice is also, of course, forever written
into Easter week by those planners of the rebellion who
chose the Christian holy season that celebrates with the
triumph of resurrection the sacrificial agony of the
crucifixion. The season of Easter is spring, and the
familiar dichotomy of death-rebirth, the red and the
green, echoes throughout the book.

Religion, Ireland, England are the large "ideas" that
the characters of the novel seek to define themselves by
and against, and the very patterns themselves become
ways of measuring the messiness, the unanswerable
frustrations, the contingent relationships of human life
against a social background. In an article entitled "A
Respect for the Contingent," Joy Rome examines *The
Red and the Green* as it takes its place in the
philosophical and literary development of Murdoch as a
novelist and rather refreshingly sees it as a part of the
total canon rather than as an obligatory "Irish" novel,
something of a sport in Murdoch's pattern of fictional

evolution. Rome's conclusion that *The Red and the Green* "may be considered one of the major works of the Murdoch canon, [for] she has successfully combined the seemingly imcompatible techniques of naturalism and allegory, thereby capturing 'the substantial, impenetrable, individual, indefinable and valuable' in man, that represents for her his reality" *(English Studies in Africa* [March 1971]) pushes the case too far, but correctly insists that *The Red and the Green* ought to be read within the context of Murdoch's other work.

The characters in *The Red and the Green* may seem at first glance a more tightly woven group than in some of Murdoch's other novels, but *The Bell, A Fairly Honourable Defeat, The Time of the Angels, The Italian Girl, A Severed Head, The Unicorn,* and others come immediately to mind as novels with similar closed groupings of characters. The incestuous, claustrophobic, enforced relationship and the ways in which man finds or fails to find his freedom within such contexts is a consistent area of exploration for Murdoch, and it may be that the relationships seem tighter and more clearly delineated in *The Red and the Green* simply because of Murdoch's emphasis on the Irish situation.

The "family," which is a subject of great interest to Andrew's British mother, who loved to say, "We Anglo-Irish families are so complex," is quite clearly, for purposes of the novel, a microcosmic representation of human possibilities under the added pressure of a complicated historical and political relationship. (Within the family, the relationships are even more complex than the proper Mrs. Chase-White could ever guess, and when Aunt Millicent Kinnard replies, "We're practically incestuous," it is with a knowledgeable irony that makes her comment more than symbolic.)

Within the microcosm of the family the Irish members are generally shown as more passionate, alive, and sensitive than the "British" side, capable of both greater feeling and greater folly. Insofar as Andrew and Patrick Dumay embody this dichotomy, they are reenacting the relationship of their fathers. Andrew's father, Henry Chase-White, paled in the presence of his half-brother, Brian Dumay, and even as a child Andrew suffered for his father's discomfort in the presence of the Irish relatives. Andrew early realized that his Uncle Brian was "the perfect all-around out-of-doors uncle . . . leading the way, leaping from rock to rock, followed by the shouting children," while his own father picked "his way cautiously behind." In memory Andrew sees Uncle Brian plunging with the children into the sea, while his own father sat on the shore, reading his book, forever separated from the life of nature and of the robust Irish relatives.

Andrew's fear of the life of his Irish cousins is extended to include his relationship to Frances. He identifies the sexual act with death, his own final death, and he conceives both in terms of horror and violence. His ideas about love, like his ideas about being a soldier, have been created out of a kind of British schoolboy romanticism. His relationship to Frances is best symbolized by the childhood swing he repairs for her to swing back and forth on, avoiding adult confrontation and the commitment of feeling. In fact, his relationship with her is one that he supposes he has because it is "expected." In this, as in all other relationships, he never initiates action out of his own sense of an identity beyond that of the British decency and conscientiousness expected of him by his mother. His name, "Chase-White," appropriately sums him up.

Within what seems to be almost a simplistic opposition of the reserved, sterile British and the robust, passionate Irish, there are enough variations, within the Irish characters at least, to save the book from stereotypical dullness. Health, as the general division of characters might suggest, is not all on the side of the Irish, for passion lacking fulfillment in the external world turns back upon itself in the various guises of love, and there is a certain justice in Andrew's apprehension of the family as "the snake that eats its own tail."

At one extreme within the Irish side of the family is Millicent Kinnard whose passionate nature is a terrible burden, a weapon to be used against herself and others. The question of incest aside, her playing with Andrew, Christopher Bellman, Patrick, and Barnabas, and the literal target practice in her bedroom all speak to a frustrated sexuality, a passion without object until Millie discovers Pat Dumay's passion for Ireland, a passion which is so great and so pure that he, rather than Millie, becomes the real object of the love of the other characters.

Pat Dumay loves only two things: his brother Cathal and the idea of Ireland's freedom, both of which are identified for him with death. The unhealthy narcissism of Pat's love, written clearly in his hatred of women and his visits to Dublin's prostitutes as acts of willful degradation, is complemented by his unbridled love for his brother Cathal, that youthful mirror image of himself. He must even view Millie as "a kind of degraded boy" before he can seek her bed. When he ponders the problem of keeping his brother out of harm's way on the day of the fighting, he considers as one alternative a solution recommended by its uniting of death with love:

> the thought [came] that he would kill Cathal. . . . That would make him entirely safe. If Cathal were dead he would be beyond harm, and tomorrow Pat would be free to die himself. Was that not, after all, the best thing? He loved Cathal too much to allow him to be hurt by anyone else.

Despite Pat's rejection of the easy sentimentality of seeing Ireland as Cathleen ni Houlihan, he finds in his country the dark bride who can provide him the purity not possible in mortal woman and at the same time offer him the opportunity to make the final sacrifice through suffering, to lose that gross and mortal self in a pure act of will. "His Ireland was nameless, a pure Ireland of the mind, to be relentlessly served by a naked sense of justice and a naked self-assertion. There were in his drama only these two characters, Ireland and himself." Pat Dumay's asceticism finds its perfection in death, and in its service of Ireland, a Holy Death. Ireland is the crucible in which he will try his soul. It is this hard strength, bought at such a price, that makes him so attractive to the other characters, who cannot find in the pattern of history a way to give meaning to their lives.

Barnabas Drumm is almost a parody of Pat, his stepson, and in some ways almost a caricature of Irish characteristics. Barney is a failed priest, a man whose orders are denied him because he allows Millie to enslave his affections to the extent that even when he knows she has played with him and cast him off, he becomes her creature, her fool. Ironically, after his rejection by the order, he does lead an ascetic's life, for he never consummates his marriage to his long-suffering wife, Kathleen Kinnard. He spends his days supposedly at work on the Lives of the Irish Saints but actually on a self-justifying document of his life with Kathleen. He drags out his days between the pub and the library, ridden by guilt and failure of nerve, hiding behind the elaborate mechanisms of his romantic escapes. He is, in some ways, Pat Dumay grown old, Pat without purpose, a spelling out of what Pat might have become without Easter week—without the purpose and the period of his life. The dark, mysterious currents of Irish life, which Andrew Chase-White so much fears, have in Barney been reduced to stagnant pools, although the reader needs to remember that Barney's Irishness, like his Catholicism, is his, to some extent, by adoption. He is one of those Anglo-Irish with "a strong peppering of Irish patriotism in his blood," but in the last anslysis, Barney is a confirmation of what his sister, Hilda Chase-White, sees as Irishness.

If in the feelings of Andrew Chase-White and his mother toward Ireland and the Irish there is a good deal that is reminiscent of the world of *A Passage to India,* Christopher Bellman is the Fielding of Murdoch's novel. English by birth, he is an "Irish 'enthusiast' in a way which sufficiently marked him as an alien." He does not, like Barney, try to make himself Irish, but rather brings to Ireland an imaginative sympathy for her history, people, and politics. If there is, in all the many "discussions" about Ireland in the novel, a sensible but sensitive point of view, it belongs to Bellman. Even though he is mistaken in believing that there will be no "trouble" in Ireland (". . . what trouble could the Irish make, even if they wanted to? They've got no arms and they're not insane."), he alone among the "English" characters understands Casement's motives. It is Beliman who delivers the judgment about Roger Casement which might well be Pat Dumay's epitaph:

> "It's the old story. 'England's difficulty is Ireland's opportunity.' Casement belongs to a classical tradition. And in a way I can't help admiring the fellow. It must be a lonely, bitter business out there in Germany. He's a brave man and a patriot. He does it purely for love of Ireland. To love Ireland so much, to love anything so much, even if he's wrong headed, is somehow noble."

Christopher Bellman, finally, on April 27, 1916, is killed in Dublin as he tries to make his way into the Post Office to join with the Irish in their "insane" heroism. The source of the shot which kills him is unknown: it could have come from either side. In the one irrational act of his life (in his pursuit of Millie he has never been deceived about her motives), he pays a high price when he attempts to join the men in the Post Office. The narrative pattern of the novel would tend to bear out Andrew's dark fear of the irrational attraction of Ireland.

The "survivors" of the Easter Rising are two: Frances and Kathleen. (Millie is still alive, "living" in the glory of the bandages she had rolled during the fighting, but she is not a survivor. She is wreckage cast up out of Easter week.) Frances and Kathleen survive perhaps because they have in common a practical concern for humanity and an ability to adapt to necessity. The cost of Frances's survival has been to make her life in England with a sardonic English husband, keeping deeply secret the real life of the self:

> She did not really think all that much about the old days; and yet now for a moment it seemed to her that these thoughts were always with her, and that she had lived out, in those months, in those weeks, the true and entire history of her heart, and that the rest was a survival. Of course this was unfair to her children and to the man with whom she had journeyed so far into this workaday middle of her life.

Part of that workaday journey involves listening to and mediating her husband's sarcastic remarks about Ireland, which he sees as a rainy "provincial dump living on German capital. A dairy-farming country that can't even invent its own cheese." Quite confident that he and England are part of the mainstream of the world, he finds "Cathleen ni Houlihan . . . a great bore," a land of "pure bloody-minded Romanticism, the sort of thing that makes people into Fascists nowadays."

No one knows better than Frances the cost of the Irish heroism of Easter week: the deaths of her father and Pat Dumay, and of Cathal Dumay in the unfinished business of the Irish Civil War. Yet with all her knowledge, she can speak to the beauty of sacrifice, can acknowledge the gain to come out of the loss of the Rising.

The reader is perhaps most surprised to hear Frances insist to her son that Andrew Chase-White "wasn't English, he was Irish." His death had come not in Dublin but at Passchendaele, Belgium, in 1917 (and with it an M.C.), and every event in the novel seems to have made him "English," from his fear of his Irish cousins to his commission in the English cavalry. As we have seen, he had been a man fearful of experience, of the passionate life, and yet on the day of the Rising he learned and acknowledged the depth of his love for Pat Dumay. Perhaps it is his belated capacity to feel and his final heroism at Passchendaele that mark him as "Irish" in Frances's mind, but for the reader, her epithet, which is meant to be a salute, remains wholly gratuitous.

The overstatement of the Irish cause which Frances makes in the epilogue is somewhat balanced by the letter she receives from Kathleen, the other "survivor." Kathleen's letter speaks to the reality of the situation and implicitly balances out Frances's uncharacteristic romanticism. An English major has been living in the Dumay house, although now he is a welcome guest, paying rent, and an English family has bought the Chase-White house. Kathleen makes it clear that Ireland is free now but that that freedom implies an accommodation of the English that was never a part of the rhetoric of a Pat or Cathal Dumay. Kathleen's letter, which begins this last section, is not, however, effective in mitigating the romantic force of the whole section.

That Murdoch felt a need to add the epilogue to this novel and that it should seek to give a measure of distanced meaning to the events of Easter week seems strange even beyond the necessities of *The Red and the Green* as a novel, for it is not like Murdoch as a novelist to accept romanticized absolutes about historical events or to see value in such judgments. The familiar irony and distance which have characterized the rest of this novel (and the rest of the Murdoch cannon) are gone, and one must conclude, finally, that perhaps, in some more basic sense than Murdoch had in mind, the Irish would not be denied.

3

The Irish Connection

The question of Iris Murdoch's Irishness is one that must, inevitably, be confronted in a series on Irish writers. And whatever answers are given will be, at best, less than satisfactory. The question of birth aside (for if this were the only consideration, Mary Lavin would be a New England writer, Doris Lessing, Rhodesian, etc.), the real question would seem to be about the writer's own consciousness of national materials and (more or less) conscious attitudes toward them. In this respect, the reader quickly notices the persistence of Irish characters in Murdoch's novels—the lower-class characters often touched with a chameleon-like nature, the middle-class or Anglo-Irish characters with a capacity for introspective sensitivity.

Aside from the characters of *The Red and the Green,* whose nationality is geographically predetermined to a large extent, the Irish character shows up as the servant in middle-class English society, a servant who is almost a stock character in several of the novels—a character on whom colorfulness is conferred automatically as an attribute of his Irishness. *Under the Net* and *The Nice and the Good* both have the Irish manservant who has a certain easygoing casualness, shrewdness, and sexual attractiveness which seem to come with his national origin. Fivey, who, in *The Nice and the Good,* is able, chameleon-like, to satisfy everyone's notion of what an Irishman *ought* to be like, succeeds in carrying off Welsh Judy, the statuesque Celtic "Helen of Troy," in a neat and ironic national packaging of characters at the same time that he indulges in the petty thievery appropriate to such a character and makes off with some of his employer's more cherished jewelry.

In some cases the servant class in Murdoch's novels provide interesting and complex characters, as in *The Unicorn,* but her lower-class Irish characters are, for the most part, delightful and deceptively simple. In other words, their Irishness operates as a kind of novelistic shorthand, a way of defining certain expectations. In the sense that simplicity is a part of the definition, Patti O'Driscoll, the lonely, half-Irish black servant of *The Time of the Angels,* qualifies, although one suspects that her Irishness is a way of enforcing the reader's view of her as a displaced person, one of the world's castaways. That the idea of Irishness in the English world of Murdoch's novels carries with it a class status is reinforced by the Italian servant girls of *The Italian Girl,* who are indiscriminately called by the common Irish name Maggie. The decadence and inhumanity of the Narraways is made clear in the novel in a number of ways, and surely this unthinking stereotyping of the long succession of Italian girls is one of them, and one that makes an oblique comment on English-Irish relations.

In *The Sandcastle,* Murdoch makes Tim Burke, the goldsmith and liberal politician with his name straight out of Synge's plays, again an easygoing, generous, whiskey-drinking Irishman with an eye for the ladies. He is more complex a character, however, than the Irish servants who remain unknowable to the middle-class English or Anglo-Irish characters of the novels, for the reader experiences a sense of his intuitive courtesy and robust potential for making things happen, which is played off against the colorless and will-less Mor, in an opposition of Irish-English attributes to be explored more fully by Murdoch in *The Red and the Green.* For Mor, whose most imaginative act before he meets Rain Carter has been to name his Golden Retriever Liffey, Tim represents an affection, warmth, and vitality he has not found in his own life. When Tim declares his own love for the constricted Nan, Mor's wife, he offers as proof of his affection a desire to share with her "Things about Ireland, about when I was a child there, things I couldn't tell to anybody else," as if he could warm her cold English conventionality with things Irish.

The Anglo-Irish protagonist of *A Severed Head* belongs to a different class structure altogether. Yet when Martin Lynch-Gibbon sets out on the "difficult" task of describing himself, he notes immediately that he comes on his "father's side of an Anglo-Irish family. My clever artistic mother was Welsh. I have never lived in Ireland, though I retain a sentimental sense of connection with that poor bitch of a country." Lynch-Gibbon, whose name seems an ironic invitation to the action of the novel, is as condescendingly superior about his emotional life as he is about Ireland, and the reader suspects that his Anglo-Irish birth serves primarily to mark his general separation from experience and his sentimental connection with all the facets of his life.

The same kind of sentimental condescension is spelled out specifically toward the Irish serving class in *The Nice and the Good* when Kate Gray invades Fivey's kitchen and feels immediately a kind of primitive sexual attraction. On discovering that they are both from County Clare, she categorizes him at once as "A real child of nature . . . very simple and moving . . . , a true peasant." He is, for her, a warm and "beastlike presence," a "marvelous animal . . . straight out of the Irish countryside," and with this realization of Fivey, she proceeds to exercise *le droit de "seigneuse"* for a moment's excitement on a dull London afternoon.

Strange as it seems to be discussing traditional class structure in the work of a contemporary novelist, class differentiation does appear in Murdoch's novels whenever the Irish appear, and the attitudes and assumptions involved are a part of the basic fabric of life for those good, upper-middle-class English or Anglo-Irish people who hold them. Kate Gray, who sees herself as quite liberal and enlightened regarding such questionable subjects as infidelity and homosexuality, never for a moment questions her preconceptions about Fivey, the simple animal, any more than the enlightened white women of Ralph Ellison's *Invisible Man* question their ideas about the animal sexuality of black males. This whole incident in Kate Gray's life becomes a comment on the rational, sensible, jolly relationship which she has

with her husband Octavian, and it provides, the reader
suspects, a more accurate key to her character than to
Fivey's, which seems not to be at issue at all. Yet the
novel, in showing Fivey absconding with Judy and the
jewelry, bears out the stereotype of the Irish character,
which Murdoch has used earlier to make her ironic
comment aimed at Kate Gray. The treatment of the
Irish and Anglo-Irish in Murdoch's novels suggests at
best a certain ambivalence on the part of the author, an
ambivalence which she has tried to confront, without
complete success, in *The Red and the Green.*

In *Under the Net,* which has been characterized as
one of Murdoch's "London" novels, the protagonist is,
once again, Anglo-Irish, and his companion-manservant
is characteristically Irish. Jake Donoghue, like Lynch-
Gibbon, begins his account of himself with the notation
that he is Irish only in a passing connection. He
admonishes the reader: "My name is James Donoghue,
but you needn't bother about that as I was in Dublin
only once, on a whiskey blind, and saw daylight only
twice, when they let me out of Store Street police
station, and then when Finn put me on the boat for
Holyhead." The reader assumes that Donoghue is Anglo-
Irish because at the end of the novel Finn's religion is
used to mark the insurmountable gulf between the two
of them, and in the shorthand of Murdoch's canon, to
be Protestant is to be Anglo-Irish or English.

Finn (Peter O'Finney), who claims to be Donoghue's
remote cousin, has the instinctual Irish casualness so
accentuated by its contrast to the more cerebral English.
As a character, Finn is more completely drawn than
Murdoch's other lower-class Irish characters. Donoghue

says of their complicated relationship, "He isn't exactly my servant. He seems often more like my manager." Finn has an existence beyond the Irish stereotype, although when he becomes self-proclaimedly Irish in his letter at the end of the novel, he begins to sound like the stereotype he has so narrowly escaped to that point. He tells Jake that he has gone Home: "I'll be in Dublin now and the Pearl Bar will always find me. . . . Hoping to see you when you come over to the Emerald Isle." Donoghue knows he can never accept Finn's invitation to Dublin, for Finn is now at home, and even the perpetual parasite, Jake, would be too acutely aware of his role as the visitor, the disinherited Anglo-Irishman who can't go home again. Finn in Dublin is no longer one of the displaced persons of the world. As long as they had lived by their wits, parasites on the modern city and its vanities, a relationship has been possible, but the Irishman at home has moved into his own world. As Mrs. Tinckham observes vaguely but not particularly cryptically about the totality of Finn's homegoing, "there's always religion."

The persistent use of Irish characters, even as seen by the English or ascendancy characters as stereotypes, suggests Murdoch's awareness of "Irishness" as a defining quality of life, however partially she may, as a novelist, have been able to apprehend and portray that quality. It is in connection with a different kind of character that Iris Murdoch has been accused of being an Anglo-Irish snob by Gabriel Pearson ("Iris Murdoch and the Romantic Novel," *New Left Review* [January-April 1967]), who finds her treatment of Honor Klein's "Jewish characteristics" in *A Severed Head* "the pro-

duct of an odd sort of inverted Anglo-Irish snobbery."
The snobbery diagnosed in the case of Honor Klein is
set within the context of a larger group of characters by
another unfriendly critic, Linda Kuehl, who notes a
strain of general Anglo-Saxon superiority in Murdoch's
"equation of the foreigner [in general] and supernat-
uralism on the one hand and the Englishman and
pragmatism on the other." If this snobbery is to be
fairly assessed in Murdoch's treatment of "foreign"
characters, it must be extended to her Irish characters
(with the notable exception of *The Red and the Green),*
although the Irish characters are almost always reduced
by a lower class association that denies them the
achieved control of an Honor Klein or Mischa Fox. Is it
naturalistic detail or a self-conscious protective device
which makes it possible to reduce MacMurraghue,
Fellow and Tutor in philosophy in *An Accidental Man,*
by virtue of a gratuitous reference to nationality:
"MacM. is back with his old ma and full of Irish gloom.
He requests us to kick the Pope on our return journey"?
And in the same novel, as a piece of descriptive
domestic English scene, Murdoch notes in detail, "The
Irishman, with a long shadow . . . clipping the lawn."

It is difficult to know with what degree of consciousness Murdoch expresses the attitudes implied in details
like these, but one suspects that the same high degree of
awareness and sensitivity that she brings to her delinea-
tion of social attitudes and interactions in general is at
work here and that details like these are meant to work
primarily as criticisms of an unthinking and callow
English society—at least, this is the most charitable
interpretation that can be put upon the matter.

A less specific kind of character in the Murdoch novels may have Irish associations insofar as the gothic embraces certain aspects of the Irish literary tradition in writers such as Maria Edgeworth or Sheridan LeFanu. The influence of LeFanu, specifically on *The Unicorn,* has been pointed out by Murdoch herself and examined in detail by several critics, but given the catholic range of Murdoch's sources and allusions, it is hard to attach too much significance to her use of this little-read Irish writer. Despite its specific references to the work of LeFanu, *The Unicorn* owes as much in general atmosphere to the tradition of *Wuthering Heights* or even to some of Hardy's novels, although the setting itself becomes in Murdoch a part of the ironic comment she makes about the gothic mode as a solution to the problem of existence.

The Red and the Green, as one would expect, is the novel which most directly shows the influence of specific Irish works of literature. The importance of the general context of Yeats's "Easter 1916" has been discussed, and in his study of influences, Howard German explores at length some of the many other Irish sources. Swift, Gogarty, George Moore, Yeats, and Joyce are a part of the texture of this novel—acknowledgment by Iris Murdoch of her debt to the perceptions of Ireland's modern writers.

It is not the matter of specific Irish writers which is finally of greatest importance in trying to assess Murdoch's debt to her Irish connection; it is, rather, in the less definable and demonstrable matters of her use of setting, her sense of the value of individual difference in characters, and her tolerance for and use of eccentricity as a way of achieving individual difference in a world of reductively dreary sameness. It is only sensible to acknowledge at once that any one of these aspects of Murdoch's work could have come to her from other sources, and, perhaps, ultimately did, but there is the inescapable fact that these aspects are strong indeed in the work and attitudes of those writers from Swift to Yeats who formed the modern Irish consciousness.

Murdoch uses setting for effect more unabashedly than most modern writers, except perhaps American Southern writers (who have their affinities with Irish writers), and while it is certainly true that a nineteenth-century English writer like Scott, whom Murdoch cites with approval in another context, could have provided her with her model for settings, it could have come as well out of the Irish literary tradition. In her penchant for the extremes of pastoral sunshine and gothic mists, for example, the influence could easily have been the Synge of *In the Shadow of the Glen, The Well of the Saints,* or *Deirdre of the Sorrows.* The perhaps overcareful emphasis upon the rain in *The Red and the Green* and the setting of Gaze Castle in *The Unicorn* are two cases which can be set beside the pastoral moment of the sunlit meadow in *The Sandcastle*—a moment which, insofar as versions of pastoral cannot be sustained, is quickly undercut by the weight of a real world in which expensive motor cars slowly but inexorably overturn to settle on their tops in crystal-clear rivers.

Equally difficult to establish with absolute certainty but coincidental enough to bear consideration is the insistence by Murdoch on eccentricity, the exaggeration of character and gesture which is everywhere in the Irish literary tradition. Again, it is clear that Murdoch's model might be elsewhere—in Dickens, perhaps, but in the use Murdoch makes of eccentricity for mounting an attack on the comfortable veneer of middle-class life the echoes are those of Synge or Yeats, O'Casey or Joyce. Yet there is in Murdoch none of the rage associated with such attacks in these writers. Although her mode is also comedy, an ironic detachment like that Murdoch so admires in certain nineteenth-century English writers is a fact that makes it difficult to push too hard an exclusive claim of Irish influence in the treatment of character. Murdoch's eclecticism makes it difficult to speak of her solely within the Irish context, and yet it virtually guarantees that the force of her Irish background is to be felt, if only indirectly. It does seem unlikely that Iris Murdoch's own contribution, to date at least, will much affect future readings of the meaning of Irish experience, but it is certain that, insofar as her own work grows out of Irish influences, implicit and explicit, she is an important contemporary writer to students of Irish literature.

Selected Bibliography

PRINCIPAL WORKS OF IRIS MURDOCH

The Accidental Man. London and New York, 1971.
"Against Dryness: A Polemical Sketch." *Encounter* 16 (January 1961): 16-20.
The Bell. London and New York, 1958.
The Black Prince. London and New York, 1973.
Bruno's Dream. London and New York, 1969.
"The Darkness of Practical Reason." *Encounter* 27 (July 1966): 46-50.
"The Existentialist Hero." *The Listener* 43 (March 23, 1950): 523-24.
A Fairly Honourable Defeat. London and New York, 1970.
The Flight from the Enchanter. London and New York, 1956.
"Hegel in Modern Dress." *The New Statesman and Nation* 53 (May 25, 1957): 675.
"A House of Theory," in Norman Mackenzie, ed., *Conviction* (London, 1958), pp. 218-33; reprinted in *Partisan Review* 26 (Winter 1959): 17-31.
"The Idea of Perfection." *The Yale Review* 53 (March 1964): 342-80.
The Italian Girl. London and New York, 1964.
"Knowing the Void." *Spectator* 197 (November 2, 1956): 613-14.
"Mass, Might and Myth." *Spectator* 209 (September 7, 1962): 337-38.

"Metaphaysics and Ethics," in D. F. Pears, ed., *The Nature of Metaphysics* (London, 1957); pp. 99-123.

The Nice and the Good. London and New York, 1968.

"Nostalgia for the Particular." *Proceedings of the Aristotelian Society* 52 (1952): 243-60.

"The Novelist as Metaphysician." *The Listener* 43 (March 16, 1950): 473, 476.

The Red and the Green. London and New York, 1965.

The Sandcastle. London and New York. 1957.

Sartre: Romantic Rationalist. New Haven, 1953.

A Severed Head. London and New York, 1961.

"The Sublime and the Beautiful Revisted." *The Yale Review* 49 (December 1959): 247-71.

"The Sublime and the Good." *Chicago Review* 13 (Autumn 1959): 42-55.

The Time of the Angels. London and New York, 1966.

"T. S. Eliot As a Moralist," in Neville Braybrooke, ed., *T. S. Eliot: A Symposium for His Seventieth Birthday* (New York, 1958), pp. 152-60.

Under the Net. London and New York, 1954.

The Unicorn. London and New York, 1963.

An Unofficial Rose. London and New York, 1962.

"Vision and Choice in Morality." *Aristotelian Society: Dreams and Self-knowledge,* Supplementary Vol. 30 (1956): 32-58.

CRITICAL STUDIES

Allen, Walter. *The Modern Novel in Britain and the United States.* New York, 1964.

Allsop, Kenneth. *The Angry Decade: A Survey of the Cultural Revolt of the Nineteen-Fifties.* London, 1958.

Balakian, Nona. "The Flight from Innocence: England's Newest Literary Generation." *Books Abroad* 33 (Summer 1959): 261-70.

Baldanza, Frank. "Iris Murdoch and the Theory of Personality." *Criticism* 7 (Spring 1965): 176-89.

–––. "The Nice and the Good." *Modern Fiction Studies* 15 (Autumn 1969): 417-28.

Barrows, John. "Living Writers–7: Iris Murdoch." *John O'London's* 4 (May 4, 1961): 498.

Berthoff, Warner. "Fortunes of the Novel: Muriel Spark and Iris Murdoch." *Massachusetts Review* 8 (Spring 1967): 301-32.

Bradbury, Malcolm. "Iris Murdoch's *Under the Net.*" *Critical Quarterly* 4 (Spring 1962): 47-54.

Byatt, A. S. *Degrees of Freedom: The Novels of Iris Murdoch.* London and New York, 1965.

Dick, Bernard F. "The Novels of Iris Murdoch: A Formula for Enchantment." *Bucknell Review* 14 (May 1966): 66-81.

Felheim, Marvin. "Symbolic Characterization in the Novels of Iris Murdoch." *Texas Studies in Literature and Language* 2 (Summer 1960): 189-97.

Fraser, G. S. "Iris Murdoch and the Solidity of the Normal." *International Literary Annual* 2 (1959): 37-54.

German, Howard. "Allusions in the Early Novels of Iris Murdoch." *Modern Fiction Studies* 15 (Autumn 1969): 361-77.

–––. "The Range of Allusions in the Novels of Iris Murdoch." *Journal of Modern Literature* 2 (September 1971): 57-85.

Gindin, James. "Images of Illusion in the Work of Iris Murdoch." *Texas Studies in Language and Literature* 2 (Summer 1960): 180-88.

–––. *Postwar British Fiction: New Accents and Attitudes.* Berkeley and Los Angeles, 1962.

Goldberg, Gerald Jay. "The Search for the Artist in Some Recent British Fiction. *South Atlantic Quarterly* 62 (Summer 1963): 387-401.

Hall, James. *The Tragic Comedians: Seven Modern British Novelists.* Bloomington, Ind., 1963.

Hall, William F. *"Bruno's Dream:* Technique and Meaning in the Novels of Iris Murdoch." *Modern Fiction Studies* 15 (Autumn 1969): 429-43.

–––. " 'The Third Way': The Novels of Iris Murdoch." *Dalhousie Review* 46 (Autumn 1966): 306-18.

Heyd, Ruth. "An Interview with Iris Murdoch." *University of Windsor Review* 1 (Spring 1965): 142.

Hoffman, Frederick J. "Iris Murdoch: The Reality of Persons." *Critique* 7 (Spring 1964): 48-57.

———. "The Miracle of Contingency: The Novels of Iris Murdoch." *Shenandoah* 17 (Autumn 1965): 49-56.

Hope, Francis. "The Novels of Iris Murdoch." *London Magazine* 1 (August 1961): 84-87.

Jones, Dorothy. "Love and Morality in Iris Murdoch's *The Bell.*" *Meanjin Quarterly* 26 (1966): 85-90.

Kaehele, Sharon, and German, Howard. "The Discovery of Reality in Iris Murdoch's *The Bell.*" *PMLA* 82 (December 1967): 554-63.

Kemp, Peter. "The Fight Against Fantasy: Iris Murdoch's *The Red and the Green.*" *Modern Fiction Studies* 15 (Autumn 1969), 403-15.

Kenney, Alice P. "The Mythic History of *A Severed Head.*" *Modern Fiction Studies* 15 (Autumn 1969): 387-401.

Kermode, Frank. "The House of Fiction: Interviews with Seven English Novelists." *Partisan Review* 30 (Spring 1963): 61-82.

Kriegel, Leonard. "Iris Murdoch: Everybody Through the Looking-Glass." *Contemporary British Novelists,* ed. Charles Shapiro. Carbondale, Ill., 1965.

Kuehl, Linda. "Iris Murdoch: The Novelist as Magician/The Magician as Artist." *Modern Fiction Studies* 15 (Autumn 1969), 347-60.

Maes-Jelinek, Hena. "A House for Free Characters: The Novels of Iris Murdoch." *Revue des langues vivantes* 29 (1963): 45-69.

Martin, Graham. "Iris Murdoch and the Symbolist Novel." *British Journal of Aesthetics* 5 (July 1965): 296-300.

Martz, Louis L. "Iris Murdoch: The London Novels." *Twentieth-Century Literature in Retrospect (Harvard English Studies 2),* ed., Reuben A. Brower. Cambridge, Mass., 1970, pp. 65-86.

McCarthy, Mary. "Characters in Fiction." *Partisan Review* 28 (March-April 1961): 171-91.

McDowell, Frederick P. W. " 'The Devious Involutions of Human Character and Emotions': Reflections on Some Recent British Novels." *Wisconsin Studies in Contemporary Literature* 4 (Autumn 1963): 339-66.

Mehta, Ved. *The Fly and the Fly-Bottle: Encounters with British Intellectuals.* Boston, 1963.

Meidner, O. M. "The Progress of Iris Murdoch." *English Studies in Africa* 4 (March 1961): 17-38.

―――. "Reviewer's Bane: A Study of Iris Murdoch's *The Flight from the Enchanter.*" *Essays in Criticism* 11 (1961): 435-47.

Mercier, Vivien. "Arrival of the Anti-Novel." *The Commonweal* 30 (May 8, 1959): 149-51.

Murray, William M. "A Note on the Iris Murdoch Manuscripts in the University of Iowa Libraries." *Modern Fiction Studies* 15 (Autumn 1969): 445-48.

O'Connor, William Van. "Iris Murdoch: *A Severed Head.*" *Critique* 5 (1962): 74-77.

―――. *The New University Wits and the End of Modernism.* Carbondale, Ill., 1963.

O'Sullivan, Kevin. "Iris Murdoch and the Image of Liberal Man." *Yale Literary Magazine* 131 (December 1962): 27-36.

Pearson, Gabriel. "Iris Murdoch and the Romantic Novel." *New Left Review* 13-14 (January-April 1962): 137-45.

Pondrom, Cyrena Norman. "Iris Murdoch: *The Unicorn.*" *Critique* 6 (Winter 1963): 177-80.

Porter, Raymond J. *"Leitmotiv* in Iris Murdoch's *Under the Net."* *Modern Fiction Studies* 15 (Autumn 1969): 379-85.

Rabinovitz, Rubin. *Iris Murdoch.* New York, 1968.

Raymond, John. "The Unclassifiable Image." *New Statesman* 56 (November 15, 1958): 697-98.

Rome, Joy. "A Respect for the Contingent: A Study of Iris Murdoch's Novel *The Red and the Green."* *English Studies in Africa* 14 (March 1971): 87-98.

Scholes, Robert. "Iris Murdoch's 'Unicorn.' " *The Fabulators.* New York, 1967.

Souvage, Jacques. "Symbol as Narrative Device: An Interpretation of Iris Murdoch's *The Bell."* *English Studies* 43 (April 1962): 81-96.

―――. "Theme and Structure in Iris Murdoch's *The Flight from the Enchanter."* *Spieghel Historiael van de Bond van Gentste Germanisten* 3 (1960-61): 73-88.

———. "The Unresolved Tension: An Interpretation of Iris Murdoch's *Under the Net.*" *Revue des langues vivantes* 26 (1960): 420-30.

Thomson, P.W. "Iris Murdoch's Honest Puppetry—The Characters of *Bruno's Dream.*" *Critical Quarterly* 11 (Autumn 1969): 277-83.

Tracy, Honor. "Misgivings about Miss Murdoch." *The New Republic* 151 (October 10, 1964): 21-22.

Vickery, John B. "The Dilemmas of Language: Sartre's *La Nausée* and Iris Murdoch's *Under the Net.*" *Journal of Narrative Techniques* 1 (May 1971): 69-76.

Wall, Stephen. "The Bell in *The Bell.*" *Essays in Criticism* 13 (July 1963): 265-73.

Weatherhead, A. K. "Background with Figures in Iris Murdoch." *Texas Studies in Literature and Language* 10 (Winter 1969): 635-48.

West, Paul. *The Modern Novel.* London, 1963.

Whiteside, George. "The Novels of Iris Murdoch." *Critique* 7 (Spring 1964): 27-47.

Widmann, R. L. "An Iris Murdoch Checklist." *Critique* 10 (1967): 17-29.

———. "Murdoch's *Under the Net:* Theory and Practice of Fiction." *Critique* 10 (1967): 5-17.

Wolfe, Peter *The Disciplined Heart: Iris Murdoch and Her Novels.* Columbia, Mo., 1966.